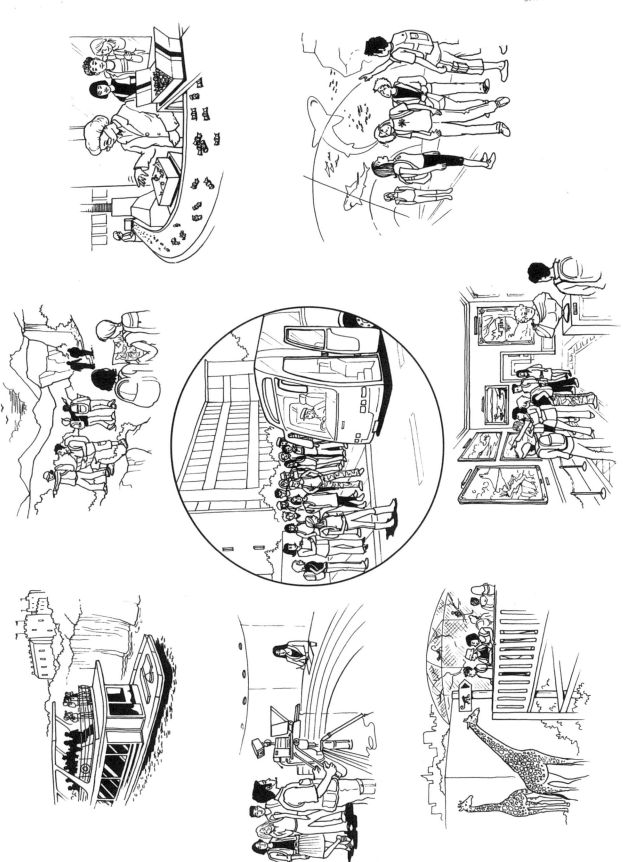

Photo A

Speaking Test Preparation Pack for

Preliminary English Test for Schools

Acknowledgements

Cambridge ESOL is grateful to the following for permission to reproduce photographs:

Part 3
Photos B and C: Getty Images

University of Cambridge ESOL Examinations
1 Hills Road
Cambridge
CB1 2EU
UK

www.CambridgeESOL.org

© UCLES 2009
It would normally be necessary to obtain written permission in advance from the publisher before photocopying any part of this book. However, the Student Worksheet pages in this book are designed to be copied and distributed in class: for these pages the normal requirements are waived here and it is not necessary to contact UCLES for permission for an individual teacher to make copies for use within his or her own classroom. Only those Student Worksheet pages which carry the wording '© UCLES 2009 Photocopiable' may be copied.

First published 2009

Project managed by Cambridge Publishing Management Ltd

Printed in the United Kingdom by Océ (UK) Ltd

ISBN 978-1-906438-59-3

Contents

Introduction

This *Speaking Test Preparation Pack for PET for Schools* has been specially created to help you to prepare your students for the Speaking test (Paper 3) of the Preliminary English Test (PET) for Schools from Cambridge ESOL. Written by experienced Speaking test examiners, it consists of:
- a book containing comprehensive Teacher's Notes and a set of eight Student Worksheets that provide detailed practice for all parts of the PET for Schools Speaking test
- candidate visuals to allow you and your students to practise with realistic visual stimuli
- a DVD showing real students taking a Speaking test to give your students a clear idea of what to expect on the day.

The Student Worksheets can be photocopied to use in class, or printed from the files on the DVD if you prefer. They cover the four parts of the Speaking test in detail and contain a variety of exercises and discussion tasks using the DVD.

The Teacher's Notes for each worksheet explain how to conduct each activity and provide answers to and commentary on the various exercises. There are also 'Teaching Tips' for each of the four parts of the Speaking test, giving you extra ideas for use in class.

The DVD contains a recording of one complete PET for Schools Speaking test, along with the Student Worksheets and candidate visuals (these visuals are also included in this book).

We hope you enjoy using the *Speaking Test Preparation Pack for PET for Schools* and wish your students every success when they take the test.

Cambridge ESOL

PET for Schools Speaking test
Teacher's Notes

Aims of the DVD and worksheets

- to raise students' awareness of the format of the PET for Schools Speaking test
- to focus students' attention on techniques that will improve their performance
- to provide opportunities for students to practise the language used in the different parts of the test
- to inform teachers about the test format for the PET for Schools Speaking test
- to provide activities and teaching tips for teachers to use with examination classes.

Please note:

The DVD and worksheets are not intended as a forum for discussing grades. Although in certain questions we are asking students to look at the candidates' performance, it is with a view to improving the students' own performance and not for them to grade the candidates on the DVD.

The PET for Schools Speaking test on the DVD has been produced for teaching purposes only and is not a live exam. There are, therefore, no grades available.

■ How to use the DVD and worksheets

The Student Worksheets are at the back of this book in the section beginning on page 23. The tasks in the worksheets are to be used at your discretion to create maximum benefit for your students. The guidelines below are suggestions only.

You can use the worksheets to:
- introduce the PET for Schools Speaking test at the beginning of your course
- review or revise key points near the exam date
- focus on different parts of the test at different times according to your syllabus.

Please note:

The worksheets are not designed to be used as complete lessons of any fixed length. Make sure that your students are aware when the answers to the tasks cannot be found on the DVD.

Some of your students may find these activities challenging. If necessary, adapt or simplify the tasks and give assistance where needed.

This worksheet is based on the first phase of Part 1 of the PET for Schools Speaking test.

Begin by explaining the purpose of the DVD and that the students taking part are volunteers. Stress that these were not the students' real tests, and that no marks have been awarded for these performances. The students on the DVD make language mistakes (as you would expect at this level), but our focus is on how they do the tasks and the type of language they use to do them, rather than on the correctness of the English.

Give out Worksheet 1 and explain to the students that Part 1 of the Speaking test has two phases. This worksheet relates to the first phase, in which the examiner asks the students for basic information about themselves. Stress that answers in this part of the test are expected to be short and purely informational.

■ Task One

Play the first phase of Part 1 on the DVD (00.00–1.09). What questions does the examiner ask Esperanza and Vitor? Ask the students to listen carefully and write down the questions on their worksheets.

Answers

1. Can I have your mark sheets, please?
2. What's your name?
3. What's your surname?
4. How do you spell it?
5. Where do you live?
6. Do you study English at school?
7. Do you like it?

Explain to the students that this part of the test is the same for all candidates, so they can practise giving perfect answers.

■ Task Two

Tell the students to work with a partner and ask and answer the same questions. Remind them that these questions should have SHORT answers.

■ Task Three

This task focuses on the spelling activity. Play the first phase of Part 1 on the DVD again and focus on the spelling of Vitor's surname. (N.B. Esperanza spells her surname wrongly, so is not the focus of the activity.)

Answer (in bold)

What is Vitor's surname?	**Lustosa. L-U-S-T-O-S-A**

■ Task Four

This task gives further practice in how to pronounce letters in English. It is oral practice to be carried out in pairs.

N.B. Point out that, as in all parts of the test, different varieties of English are acceptable, e.g. British, North American, etc., provided they are used consistently throughout the test.

Tell the students to work with a partner. They should ask each other the questions on the worksheet and write down the answers.

1. What's your first name? How do you spell it?
2. Have you got a brother/sister? What's his/her name? How do you spell it?
3. What's your English teacher's surname? How do you spell it?
4. Have you got a pet? What's its name? How do you spell it?

This worksheet is based on the last phase of Part 1 of the PET for Schools Speaking test. In this phase, candidates are expected to give more extended answers. There is not a fixed number of questions, but rather a fixed period of time is allotted. So that candidates can contribute equally, there is a menu of questions from which the examiner chooses. A candidate giving one good extended answer may not get a second question, therefore, while a candidate giving very short responses may be asked two or more questions.

The activities on the worksheet encourage candidates to extend their answers in this phase.

■ Task One

This focuses on the need to extend the answer.

 1. Play the second phase of Part 1 on the DVD (01.10–02.27). Ask the students to listen for and write down the questions that the examiner asks each student.

Answers

Questions for Vitor
What's your favourite school subject? Why?
Tell us about your family.
Questions for Esperanza
Tell us about your English teacher.

2. Ask the students to work with a partner and discuss why the examiner asks Vitor a second question. Then ask the class for their opinions.

Answer

- Why does the examiner ask Vitor a second question? – Vitor is asked a further question because his first answer was rather short, whereas Esperanza gives a suitably extended response.

Point out that the examiner may ask questions with a follow-up 'Why?' or 'Tell us about…' prompts. In both cases an extended response is expected.

■ Task Two

 1. Play the second phase of Part 1 on the DVD again, including Esperanza's answer to the question about her teacher and Vitor's answer to the question about his family. Ask the students to listen and note down Esperanza and Vitor's answers in the boxes on the worksheet.

Answers

a) What three things do we find out about Esperanza's teacher?

Esperanza's teacher
She is a woman.
She teaches students in other years at her school.
She explains things very well.

b) What do we find out about Vitor's family?

Vitor's family
His family is small.
He doesn't have any brothers or sisters.
His father is separated from his mother.

2. Ask the students to work in pairs and discuss the questions on the worksheet. This activity focuses on the content of Vitor's responses.

Answers

- Which is better: Vitor's first answer about his favourite subject, or his second answer about his family? – It is anticipated that students will find Vitor's second answer more interesting because we find out more about him.
- Why? – Because he extends his answer with reasons and examples.

■ Task Three

This task gives practice in extending responses through the use of reasons and examples. The students work on their own, and choose one of the three questions asked by the examiner on the DVD. They should write down three things they would tell the examiner in the box on the worksheet.

Remind them to give general information first, followed by more detail, and to give their opinions where appropriate.

■ Task Four

Ask students to work in pairs to practise asking and answering the questions. Draw their attention to the points to remember on their worksheets and remind them that their answers should include reasons and examples.

Remember:

- These questions should have LONGER answers – give reasons and examples
- If the examiner says 'Thank you', then it's time to stop.

This worksheet is the first of two based on Part 2 of the PET for Schools Speaking test. The focus of this worksheet is on understanding the task instructions and how to approach the task.

Point out that the focus of the test now changes from examiner-led question and answer to interaction between the candidates. Bring students' attention to what the examiner says at the end of Part 1: 'In the next part you're going to talk to each other.'

Remind them that in this task it is up to them to manage the interaction. But first they must make sure they understand what it is they have to do. Remind them that the examiner will say the instructions twice – giving out the page of visuals between the two readings of the task rubric.

■ Task One

Use the page of Part 2 candidate visuals provided at the beginning of this book, or, before the lesson, print it out from the DVD and make sure you have enough copies to give one to each pair of students.

Point out to the students that the central image in the circle will help them to understand the context for the task in Part 2 of the test. The questions here are designed to encourage the students to engage with this context and make predictions about it. Tell them not to worry about the surrounding images at the moment.

Remind students to focus on the picture in the circle in the centre of the page. Tell them to talk to their partner and discuss the questions on their worksheet:
- Who can you see in the picture in the circle?
- What do you think is happening in the picture?

■ Task Two

Play the beginning of Part 2 on the DVD (02.28–03.22), showing the examiner giving the instructions for the task to Esperanza and Vitor. This exercise focuses the students' attention on the key features of this part of the test. Remind them that the task will have a context (given in the first sentence), followed by instructions to the students (given in the last sentence).

Answers (in bold)

Examiner:	A teacher wants to take her class out on an **educational visit**. She has asked the students **where** they would like to go. Talk together about the different **places** they could go and decide which would be the most **interesting**.

■ Task Three

Play the examiner giving the instructions for the Part 2 task a second time and ask the students to choose the answers to the question: 'What do you have to do in this part of the test?' from the three options given, a), b) or c).

Answers (in bold)

1. a) Talk about yourselves.
   b) Talk about the students in the picture.
   c) Talk about students in general.

2. a) Describe all the other pictures.
   b) Talk about the place in the most interesting picture.
   c) Talk about all the places in the pictures and then choose one.

Remind the students that the task is about an imaginary situation involving the people in the visuals. Students should give their opinions about what the people should do, not imagine they are the people or give their own personal preferences.

Remind them that the task begins with the words 'Talk together' and usually has two elements (talk about the options, then make a choice). This is the best way to approach the task. Remind them also that they have to talk for 2–3 minutes and to have a conversation. If they decide on the best option too soon, they will have nothing left to say.

Task Four

This exercise will help students engage with the visual material in this part of the test before they listen to the candidates on the DVD. This will help weaker students to understand what they hear.

1. Tell the students to look at all the pictures on the page and put a tick (✓) against all the places they can see.

   Answers (in bold)

a museum	a town hall
a farm	**a castle**
a cinema	**a mountain**
a factory	a theatre
a zoo	a beach
an aquarium	**a television studio**
a shop	**a boat on a lake/river**

2. Ask the students to work with a partner and discuss the questions on the worksheet.
   - Which do you think would be the most interesting place to visit?
   - Why?

This worksheet is based on Part 2 of the PET for Schools Speaking test.

■ Task One

This task focuses on the actual language that students use to do the task in Part 2 of the PET for Schools Speaking test.

Use the page of Part 2 candidate visuals provided at the beginning of this book, or, before the lesson, print it out from the DVD and make sure you have enough copies to give one to each pair of students.

 Play Part 2 on the DVD (03.23–05.31) of Esperanza and Vitor doing this task. Then ask the students to fill in the answers to the three questions on the worksheet.

Answers

Which of the places do they talk about?	They talk about the zoo, the castle, the lake, the museum and the mountain. They don't talk about all the pictures because Esperanza keeps going off topic.
Which do they think would be most interesting?	They seem to agree that the museum is not the best place, but they don't really come to a conclusion.
Do they talk about the students in the pictures or about themselves?	Vitor is talking about the students in the pictures, but Esperanza is mostly talking about her own experiences.

Point out that Vitor gives a good performance in this task. He talks about the people in the pictures and keeps bringing the discussion back to the task when Esperanza goes off topic. Esperanza also uses good language, but is harder to understand, so ask the students to focus on Vitor.

Tell students that this conversation is quite natural. Tell them to listen out for how Esperanza shows agreement and interest through what she says: finishing Vitor's sentences, adding information to what he says, etc.

■ Task Two

 Replay Part 2 on the DVD of Esperanza and Vitor doing this task. The students write down the reasons Vitor gives for visiting each place.

Answers

Place	Vitor's reasons for going there
The zoo	because the children can learn about animal habits
A trip on the lake	it's like a study tour because the people can look at the castle
The museum	the museum can be boring because the children are young
The mountain	it's an adventure

■ Task Three

This is a chance for students to do the task in Part 2 themselves, using the vocabulary that has been activated and the ideas they have seen on the DVD.

Give each pair of students a copy of the Part 2 candidate visuals. Ask them to read the points to remember on their worksheets and explain anything they don't understand.

Remember:

- Ask your partner questions
- Agree and disagree with each other
- Talk about the people in the pictures, not yourselves
- Talk about all the pictures
- Say if it is a good idea to visit each place or not
- Give reasons for what you say
- If the examiner says 'Thank you', then it's time to stop.

Remind students that Vitor gives the best performance because he gives reasons for his ideas and involves his partner in the task through his questions and responses.

Draw the students' attention to the Useful phrases section on their worksheets. Explain that they can use these phrases when doing the task in Part 2 of the Speaking test.

Ask questions	What do you think about the . . . ? What about the . . . ? Do you think the . . . is a good idea? Would the . . . be an interesting place to visit?
Agree	Yes you're right. I agree with you. I think so too.
Disagree	I don't agree. But I think the . . . is better. Maybe . . .
Give reasons	I think . . . is a good idea because . . . If they go to the . . . , they can . . .

PET for Schools Speaking test
Teacher's Notes

This worksheet is based on Part 3 of the PET for Schools Speaking test. Use Photos A and B from the candidate visuals provided at the beginning and end of this book.

■ Task One

 Play the examiner's instructions to Candidate A (05.32–06.01) and tell the students to write down the answers to the two questions on their worksheets.

Answers

1. What is the topic of the photos? – The topic is people enjoying their free time.
2. Do you talk with someone? – No. You have to talk on your own.

Explain to the students that when she says, 'Tell me what you can see in the picture', the examiner is asking for a description.

■ Task Two

1. Tell students to look at Photo A and do this task in pairs. It will help them to understand the students on the video and think about the range of possible things to describe in the picture. They list these in the box on the worksheet.

 2. Now play Part 3 on the DVD (06.02–07.06), of Esperanza describing her photograph.

The students should tick the words on their list that she mentions and add any words to their list that they haven't written down.

Answers

Place	People/Clothes	Objects	Colours	Verbs
room	two boys	instrument magazine sofa carpet lamp wall decorations books	blue white black red	sitting standing playing learning reading

■ Task Three

 Play Esperanza's description of her photograph again and tell the students to discuss the answers to the four questions in Task Three with a partner.

Answers

- Where does she begin? Why? – Esperanza begins by talking about the two boys and what they are doing. This is because they are the focus of the photograph. She then goes on to talk about the room and ends with some details of the background.

- What does she do when she doesn't know a word? – Esperanza clearly doesn't know the name of the musical instrument in English, but she talks about it nonetheless. Tell students that they are not expected to know all the vocabulary, but they are expected to keep talking. Tell them not to worry if they don't know a word, but to move on and talk about something else.

- How does she introduce her own opinions? – Esperanza doesn't only describe what she can see, but also introduces her own ideas with: 'I think it is …'. Remind students, however, that the main focus of the task is to describe what they can see. They should only add their own ideas if they are relevant to the description.

- Which two grammatical tenses does she use? Why? – Esperanza uses the simple present to describe the existence of things, e.g. objects. She uses the present continuous to talk about the activities going on in the picture.

Tell students to describe the picture as if it were happening now. If they say, for example, 'He sits on the sofa', this would be wrong as it indicates a regular habit and not a present action. 'He is sitting on the sofa' is the correct way to describe what the boy is doing.

Remind students that they don't have to use positional language (e.g. in the top left-hand corner, etc.) as this is not expected at PET level. The examiner is interested in the vocabulary that is elicited and the language used to talk about the content of the photograph (e.g. verbs, verb tenses, simple linking words).

■ Task Four

Now ask the students to look at Photo B and get them to begin to think about how to structure a description. Elicit their ideas. Encourage them to move from establishing the context to describing the main detail to describing the background detail.

1. Ask students to write down three words or phrases in the box on the worksheet.

Answers

Here are some of the answers they might write:

Place	People/Clothes	Activities
in a park under a tree on the grass outside	I can see three friends/girls. One girl is Japanese or Chinese. One girl is wearing a white skirt.	having fun talking eating having a picnic holding a blue cup drinking water

2. Ask the students to discuss with a partner:
   - Which things in the photo would you talk about first?
   - Why?

■ Task Five

 Play Vitor's description of his photo in Part 3 on the DVD (07.07–08.22). The students write down answers to the questions.

Answers

1. Does he talk about things in the same order as Esperanza does? – No. Vitor begins by establishing the context, then talking about the people who are the focus of the photo and what they are doing. Point out that Vitor soon runs out of things to say.

2. What other vocabulary would you use to talk about this picture? – Tell the students to use their vocabulary lists to think about how to extend this description. Remind them that they can talk, for example, about the ages of the people, what they are wearing and what they can see in the background.

N.B. Vitor uses the word 'hill' to mean 'park' and his pronunciation of 'city' is not very clear. He also uses a word in his own language when talking about the food. He does not describe the clothes worn.

This worksheet is based on Part 3 of the PET for Schools Speaking test. It is an extension activity that gives students a chance to describe the two photos used in the DVD in their own words and then to attempt a description of a photo they haven't heard described.

Use Photos A, B and C from the candidate visuals provided at the beginning and end of this book.

■ Task One

Students should decide who is to be Student A and who is to be Student B. Student A starts by describing Esperanza's photo (A) to their partner; then Student B describes Vitor's photo (B). Encourage the students to improve on the descriptions they have heard rather than just trying to reproduce them. Remind them to use the phrases from the worksheet to help them.

I can see . . .	There are . . .
I think it is . . . because . . .	They are . . . ing

Draw the students' attention to the points to remember on their worksheets and explain anything they don't understand.

Remember:

- Use the vocabulary that is in the picture
- Begin with the situation and then move on to the details
- Talk about the people, the activities, the objects and the background
- Use the present continuous tense to talk about the activities
- Give reasons for what you say.

Tell the students they can make notes in the boxes provided on the worksheet.

■ Task Two

1. Ask the students to look at Photo C and think about the answers to the questions. They can make notes in the box provided.

Answers

How many people are there?	There are eight people.
Where are they?	They are in a corridor, possibly in a school.
What time of day/year is it?	It is a sunny day in summertime (the students are in summer clothes), possibly lunchtime.
What are they holding/carrying?	They are holding books and files.
What are they wearing?	They are wearing casual summer clothes, shorts, jeans and T-shirts.
How do they feel?	They look relaxed and happy.

2. The students then do the task in their pairs, taking turns. They can use their answers to the six questions above to structure their descriptions. Remind students that they can use the phrases given in the 'Remember' section for Task Two on their worksheets to help them with this task.

Remember:

If you're not sure, you can give your own ideas by saying:
- I think it is . . . because . . .
- I think they are . . . because . . .

This worksheet is based on Part 4 of the PET for Schools Speaking test.

■ Task One

Play the examiner's instructions to Esperanza and Vitor (08.23–08.39) and ask the students to write down the answers to the questions on their worksheets.

Answers

1. What is the topic of Part 4? – The topic of Part 4 is free time (it follows on from the topic of the photos in Part 3).
2. Who do you talk to in Part 4? – In Part 4, the candidates talk to each other. The examiner gives the instructions at the beginning and then the candidates interact freely. The examiner may give an additional prompt, but will not ask direct questions.
3. What two things do Esperanza and Vitor have to talk about? – In this task, students have to say what they like and dislike doing in their free time.

■ Task Two

Students should discuss in pairs the following question:

• What kind of things do you think Esperanza and Vitor will talk about in this part?

Ask students to begin by writing down a list of likely topics in the box on their worksheets.

Remind them that their task begins with the words 'Talk to your partner' and usually has two elements. Remind them that they have to talk for 2–3 minutes and to have a conversation, so they should listen carefully to the examiner's instructions.

Get the students to brainstorm the types of topic that are likely to be discussed by candidates of this age group in this task. Elicit some of their ideas after the pairwork.

■ Task Three

1. Play the whole of Part 4 on the DVD (08.23–11.59) and ask the students to write down the answers to the questions on their worksheets.

Answers

a) Do they talk about the topics on your list, or different ones? – Esperanza and Vitor cover a good range of topics (computers, seeing friends, music, dance, cinema, sport, shopping, video games, etc).
b) Do they talk to each other or to the examiner? – They talk to each other and have a very good natural conversation.
c) Do they talk about themselves, or find out about their partner? – They ask each other questions and then talk about themselves in their answers. They make the conversation interesting by giving reasons and examples to illustrate what they say.
d) Why do you think the examiner gives them a new idea to talk about? – The examiner gives them new ideas to talk about because, when she asks about food, Esperanza has forgotten that the topic is free time!

2. Play the whole of Part 4 on the DVD again. While watching it, students should think about:
   • the questions Esperanza and Vitor ask each other
   • how they change topics
   • how they show interest in what their partner says
   • how they make the conversation interesting.

Tell the students to listen out for the ways in which Esperanza shows agreement and interest through what she says, e.g. finishing Vitor's sentences, adding information to what he says, laughing.

Vitor is good at asking questions that keep Esperanza on the topic and make her explain more, e.g. 'What kind of music do you like to dance to?'

Esperanza is good at asking unexpected questions, e.g. 'Do you play rugby?', that make the conversation interesting, and she's good at explaining what she means in an interesting way, e.g. 'You put the music and we dance!'

 Play Part 4 on the DVD again.

■ Task Four

Ask the students to have a similar discussion using the notes they made earlier in Task Two.

Draw students' attention to the points to remember on their worksheets and explain anything they don't understand.

Remember:
- look at each other
- ask each other questions
- show interest in what your partner says
- give examples and reasons for what you say
- give your partner a chance to speak.

Point out the Useful phrases section on the students' worksheets. Explain that they can use these phrases to help them do the task in Part 4 of the Speaking test.

Questions	I like . . . , do you? What about you? What do you think about . . . ?
Continuing the conversation	That's interesting because . . . And another thing I like is . . .
Agreeing	So do I. Me too! I agree with you about that.

Repeat the words the examiner says to Esperanza and Vitor:

Now I'd like you to talk together about your free time, and say what you like to do and what you don't like to do.

The students should talk for 3 minutes.

This worksheet is based on the whole of the PET for Schools Speaking test.

Having looked at all the parts of the PET for Schools Speaking test separately, students should now watch the whole test. Get the students to show what they have learned about the test by completing the quiz on this final worksheet as they watch.

How well do you know the PET for Schools Speaking test?

■ Task One

Maybe these issues have already been discussed in class and this task will act as a reminder, or it can be used in conjunction with written information about the test as a 'find the info' task.

Ask the students to complete Task One.

Answers (in bold)

1. How long is the Speaking test?
   A 8–10 minutes   B **10–12 minutes**   C 12–14 minutes
2. How many parts does the Speaking test have?
   A 2   B 3   C **4**
3. How many examiners are there?
   A 1   B **2**   C 3
4. How many students are there?
   A Only one   B **Usually two**   C Always three

You may wish to explain that where there is an uneven number of candidates at a centre, the final Speaking test will be a group of three rather than a pair. The group of three test is not an option for all candidates, but is only used for the last test in a session, where necessary.

■ Task Two

This is a matching exercise. Explain to the students that they need to match each part of the Speaking test (1–4) with the various things they have to do in it. They can use each letter (A–H) more than once.

> A Spell your name.
> B Talk about people in an imaginary situation.
> C Answer the examiner's questions.
> D Talk to your partner.
> E Talk about a photograph.
> F Talk about yourself.
> G Ask your partner questions.
> H Talk on your own.

Answers

Part 1. A, C, F, H
Part 2. B, D, G
Part 3. E, H
Part 4. D, F, G

You may wish at this point to explain about the reasons for a paired speaking task, and the role of the two examiners (see *PET for Schools Handbook for Teachers*, page 41).

UNIVERSITY *of* CAMBRIDGE
ESOL Examinations

PET for Schools Speaking test
Teacher's Notes

TEACHING
TIPS

■ Part 1

1. Candidates should be well prepared in the following areas:
   - basic ways of talking about the past, present and future
   - vocabulary for everyday life
     - o family
     - o daily routines
     - o future plans
     - o candidates themselves
     - o studies/home town
     - o hobbies
     - o sports
     - o likes and dislikes.

2. Give the students as many opportunities as possible to practise talking about themselves, their likes and dislikes, personal and educational background, hobbies, present circumstances, plans and hopes for the future, etc.

3. Give students practice in spelling. They will be asked to spell all or part of their name in the test.

4. Remind the students:
   - to answer the questions as fully as possible
   - to avoid long, prepared speeches
   - to extend their answers as much as possible, particularly when asked, 'Tell us about …'.

■ Part 2

1. Candidates should be well prepared in the following areas:
   - functional language for
     - o making and responding to suggestions
     - o discussing alternatives
     - o making recommendations
     - o negotiating agreement.

2. All classroom discussions in pairs and groups will provide preparation for this part of the test. Candidates should be encouraged to make positive contributions that move discussion forward by picking up on each other's ideas. Candidates should learn to discuss the situation fully with their partners, using the range of visual prompts to extend the discussion, before coming to a conclusion. It is useful to point out to candidates that if they rush to reach a conclusion too soon, opportunities to demonstrate their language skills may be lost – and it is these skills rather than the outcome of the discussion that are being assessed.

■ Part 3

1. Candidates should be well prepared in the following areas:
   - vocabulary for everyday life, e.g.
     - o colours
     - o clothes
     - o time of day
     - o weather

- language of description
  - there is/are
  - I can see
  - present continuous for activities happening at the moment
  - present simple for fact
- strategies for dealing with unknown vocabulary.

2. Remind candidates that they only need to give a simple description of what they can see in their photograph. They are not expected to speculate about the context or talk about any wider issues raised by the scenes depicted.

■ Part 4

1. Candidates should be well prepared in the following areas:
   - functional areas for
     - asking for/giving opinions
     - asking about/expressing likes and dislikes
     - asking about/expressing preferences
     - asking about/expressing habits
     - asking/talking about experiences
     - showing interest in what their partner(s) is/are saying.

2. Give students practice in giving reasons for their views and preferences, and giving examples.

3. Remind students that if they have difficulty in understanding an instruction, question or response, they should ask the examiner or their partner to repeat what was said. Marks will not normally be lost for the occasional request for repetition.

Marking and assessment

Throughout the test, candidates are assessed on their language skills, not their personality, intelligence or knowledge of the world. They must, however, be prepared to develop the conversation, where appropriate, and respond to the tasks set. Prepared speeches are not acceptable. Candidates are assessed on their own individual performance and not in relation to each other. Both examiners assess the candidates according to criteria that are interpreted at PET level.

In the PET for Schools Speaking test, candidates are examined in pairs by two examiners. One examiner (the interlocutor) directs the test. The other examiner (the assessor) takes no part in the interaction, but awards marks according to the following four analytical criteria.

■ Grammar and vocabulary

This refers to the accurate and appropriate use of grammatical forms and vocabulary. It also includes the range of both grammatical forms and vocabulary. Performance is viewed in terms of the overall effectiveness of the language used in dealing with the tasks.

■ Discourse management

This refers to the coherence, extent and relevance of each candidate's individual contribution. The candidate's ability to maintain a coherent flow of language is assessed, either within a single utterance or over a string of utterances. Also assessed here is how relevant the contributions are to what has gone before.

■ Pronunciation

This refers to the candidate's ability to produce comprehensible utterances to fulfil the task requirements. This includes stress, rhythm and intonation, as well as individual sounds. Examiners put themselves in the position of the non-language specialist and assess the overall impact of the pronunciation and the degree of effort required to understand the candidate. Different varieties of English, e.g. British, North American, Australian, etc., are acceptable, provided they are used consistently throughout the test.

■ Interactive communication

This refers to the candidate's ability to use language to achieve meaningful communication. This includes initiating and responding without undue hesitation, the ability to use interactive strategies to maintain or repair communication, and sensitivity to the norms of turn-taking.

The interlocutor gives one global mark for each candidate's performance across all parts of the test.

■ Global achievement

This refers to the candidate's overall effectiveness in dealing with the tasks in the four separate parts of the PET for Schools Speaking test. The global mark is an independent impression mark that reflects the assessment of the candidate's performance from the interlocutor's perspective.

PET for Schools Speaking test
Student Worksheets

This section contains the eight Student Worksheets for PET for Schools:
- Worksheet 1 – based on Part 1 of the Speaking test
- Worksheet 2 – based on Part 1 of the Speaking test
- Worksheet 3 – based on Part 2 of the Speaking test
- Worksheet 4 – based on Part 2 of the Speaking test
- Worksheet 5 – based on Part 3 of the Speaking test
- Worksheet 6 – based on Part 3 of the Speaking test
- Worksheet 7 – based on Part 4 of the Speaking test
- Worksheet 8 – based on the whole Speaking test

The Student Worksheet pages of this book are photocopiable and you can also print copies from the Student Worksheets folder on the DVD. For your class you will also need:
- the DVD
- for Part 2 and Part 3, the candidate visuals. You can find one set of these inside the front and back covers of this book. There is also a file on the DVD of the visual for Part 2 if you want to print more copies.

This worksheet is based on the first phase of Part 1 of the PET for Schools Speaking test.

In Part 1 of the test, you begin by giving the examiner some information about yourself.

■ Task One

Watch the beginning of Part 1 of the test on the DVD. What questions does the examiner ask Esperanza and Vitor? Write them down below.

1. _____?
2. _____?
3. _____?
4. _____?
5. _____?
6. _____?
7. _____?

■ Task Two

Now ask your partner the same questions that the examiner asks the students. Remember these questions have SHORT answers.

■ Task Three

Now watch this part of the DVD again and answer this question.
Tell your partner how you spell it.

What is Vitor's surname?	_____

■ Task Four

Practise spelling with your partner. Ask these questions and write down the answers. Then check that the spelling is correct.

1. What's your first name? How do you spell it?

   _____

2. Have you got a brother/sister? What's his/her name?
   How do you spell it?

   _____

3. What's your English teacher's surname? How do you spell it?

   _____

4. Have you got a pet? What's its name? How do you spell it?

   _____

This worksheet is based on the last phase of Part 1 of the PET for Schools Speaking test.

■ Task One

1. At the end of Part 1, the examiner asks each student a different question or questions about themselves and their lives. Watch the examiner and Vitor and write down the questions in the box below.

Questions for Vitor
_____
_____
Questions for Esperanza
_____

2. Discuss this question with a partner:
   - Why does the examiner ask Vitor a second question?

■ Task Two

1. Watch Esperanza and Vitor again.
   a) What three things do we find out about Esperanza's teacher? Write your answers in the box below.

Esperanza's teacher
_____
_____
_____

b) What do we find out about Vitor's family? Write your answers in the box below.

Vitor's family
_____
_____
_____

2. Discuss these questions with a partner.
   - Which is better: Vitor's first answer about his favourite subject, or his second answer about his family?
   - Why?

■ Task Three

Choose one of the examiner's three questions from Task One. Write down three things you would tell the examiner in the box below.

Which order will you say them in? What reasons or examples will you give?

How can you make your answer more interesting?

Question	_____ ?
My answer	_____ _____ _____

■ Task Four

Practise asking and answering the questions with your partner.

Remember:

- These questions should have LONGER answers – give reasons and examples
- If the examiner says 'Thank you', then it's time to stop.

This worksheet is based on Part 2 of the PET for Schools Speaking test.

In Part 2 of the test, you talk to your partner. The examiner tells you what to do, but does not ask you questions. You have a page of pictures to help you.

■ Task One

Look at the page of pictures your teacher will give you. These are the kinds of pictures you will have to talk about in Part 2 of the Speaking test.

In the centre of the page is a picture in a circle. Talk to your partner and discuss the following questions:
- Who can you see in the picture in the circle?
- What do you think is happening in the picture?

■ Task Two

 Now watch the examiner on the DVD giving the instructions for this part and fill in the missing words.

> *Examiner:* A teacher wants to take her class out on an _____
>
> _____ . She has asked the students _____ they would
>
> like to go. Talk together about the different _____ they
>
> could go and decide which would be the most _____ .

Were you right about the picture in the circle?

■ Task Three

 Now watch the examiner giving the instructions again.

What do you have to do in this part of the test? Choose the correct answer a), b) or c).
1. a) Talk about yourselves.
    b) Talk about the students in the picture.
    c) Talk about students in general.

2. a) Describe all the other pictures.
    b) Talk about the place in the most interesting picture.
    c) Talk about all the places in the pictures and then choose one.

■ Task Four

1. Look at all the pictures on the page and tick (✓) the places you can see.

a museum	a town hall
a farm	a castle
a cinema	a mountain
a factory	a theatre
a zoo	a beach
an aquarium	a television studio
a shop	a boat on a lake/river

2. Work with a partner and discuss the following questions:
   - Which do you think would be the most interesting place to visit?
   - Why?

This worksheet is based on Part 2 of the PET for Schools Speaking test.

■ Task One

 Watch Esperanza and Vitor on the DVD doing the task in Part 2 of the Speaking test. Write down your answers to the questions in the box below.

Which of the places do they talk about?	_____ _____ _____ _____ _____
Which do they think would be most interesting?	_____ _____
Do they talk about the students in the pictures or about themselves?	Vitor: _____ _____ Esperanza: _____ _____

■ Task Two

 Now watch this part again. What reasons does Vitor give for visiting each place?

Place	*Vitor's reasons for going there*
_____	_____
_____	_____
_____	_____
_____	_____

© UCLES 2009
PHOTOCOPIABLE

■ Task Three

Now you do the task with your partner.

Remember:

- Ask your partner questions
- Agree and disagree with each other
- Talk about the people in the pictures, not yourselves
- Talk about all the pictures
- Say if it is a good idea to visit each place or not
- Give reasons for what you say
- If the examiner says 'Thank you', then it's time to stop.

■ Useful phrases

Below are some useful phrases that may be helpful for you when doing the task in Part 2.

Ask questions	What do you think about the . . . ? What about the . . . ? Do you think the . . . is a good idea? Would the . . . be an interesting place to visit?
Agree	Yes you're right. I agree with you. I think so too.
Disagree	I don't agree. But I think the . . . is better. Maybe . . .
Give reasons	I think . . . is a good idea because . . . If they go to the . . . , they can . . .

This worksheet is based on Part 3 of the PET for Schools Speaking test.

In Part 3 of the test you talk about a photo.

Your teacher will give/show you the two photos you need for this worksheet.

■ Task One

 Listen to the examiner's instructions at the beginning of Part 3 on the DVD. Answer these two questions:

1. What is the topic of the photos?

    _____

2. Do you talk with someone?

    _____

■ Task Two

1. Look at Photo A. Work with a partner and make a vocabulary list under the headings in the box of everything you can see in the photo.

Place	People/Clothes	Objects	Colours	Verbs
____	____	____	____	____
____	____	____	____	____
____	____	____	____	____
____	____	____	____	____
____	____	____	____	____
____	____	____	____	____
____	____	____	____	____

 2. Now listen to Esperanza talking about the photograph.

Tick (✓) the words on your list that she mentions.

Add any new words she uses to your list.

■ Task Three

Now listen to Esperanza again and discuss these questions with a partner:

- Where does she begin? Why?

_____

- What does she do when she doesn't know a word?

_____

- How does she introduce her own opinions?

_____

- Which two grammatical tenses does she use? Why?

_____

■ Task Four

1. Look at Photo B. How would you begin to describe this photo? Write down three words or phrases to describe:

Place	People/Clothes	Activities
_____	_____	_____
_____	_____	_____
_____	_____	_____

2. Talk with a partner and discuss these questions:
   - Which things in the photo would you talk about first?
   - Why?

■ Task Five

Listen to Vitor describing his photo and then answer the questions below.

1. Does he talk about things in the same order?

_____

2. What other vocabulary would you use to talk about this picture?

_____

This worksheet is based on Part 3 of the PET for Schools Speaking test.

Your teacher will give/show you the photos you need for this worksheet.

■ Task One

Work with a partner and decide who is Student A and who is Student B.

1. Student A: describe Esperanza's photo to your partner. Use the phrases below to help you:

   I can see . . .

   I think it is . . . because . . .

   There are . . .

   They are . . . ing

   You can make notes in the box below if you like.

My notes

Remember:

- Use the vocabulary that is in the picture
- Begin with the situation and then move on to the details
- Talk about the people, the activities, the objects and the background
- Use the present continuous tense to talk about the activities
- Give reasons for what you say.

2. Student B: describe Vitor's photo to your partner. Use the phrases above to help you. You can make notes in the box below if you like.

My notes

© UCLES 2009
PHOTOCOPIABLE

■ Task Two

Now it's your turn to describe a picture you haven't seen before.

1. Look at Photo C. Think about the answers to the questions below. You can make notes in the box below.

How many people are there?	_____ _____
Where are they?	_____ _____
What time of day/year is it?	_____ _____
What are they holding/carrying?	_____ _____
What are they wearing?	_____ _____
How do they feel?	_____ _____

2. Now, in your pairs, take turns to describe the picture to each other. Keep talking for one minute.

Remember:

If you're not sure, you can give your own ideas by saying:
- I think it is . . . because . . .
- I think they are . . . because . . .

This worksheet is based on Part 4 of the PET for Schools Speaking test.

In Part 4 of the test, the examiner tells you what to do, but does not ask you questions. You have no pictures to help you.

■ Task One

 Listen to the examiner's instructions for Part 4 and write down the answers to the following questions.

1. What is the topic of Part 4?

   _____

2. Who do you talk to in Part 4?

   _____

3. What two things do Esperanza and Vitor have to talk about?

   _____

   _____

■ Task Two

Talk to your partner and discuss the following question:

- What kind of things do you think Esperanza and Vitor will talk about in this part?

First, make a list of possible topics in the box below, and then talk to your partner and compare.

	Esperanza	*Vitor*
Possible topics	_____ _____ _____ _____	_____ _____ _____ _____

© UCLES 2009
PHOTOCOPIABLE

■ Task Three

1. Watch Esperanza and Vitor doing the Part 4 task on the DVD and answer the following questions:

   a) Do they talk about the topics on your list, or different ones?

   _____

   b) Do they talk to each other or to the examiner?

   _____

   c) Do they talk about themselves, or find out about their partner?

   _____

   d) Why do you think the examiner gives them a new idea to talk about?

   _____

2. Now watch again and think about:
   * the questions Esperanza and Vitor ask each other
   * how they change topics
   * how they show interest in what their partner says
   * how they make the conversation interesting.

■ Task Four

Now use the notes you made earlier in Task Two to talk to your partner. Use the words and phrases in the Useful phrases box below to help you. Keep talking for 3 minutes.

Remember:
* look at each other
* ask each other questions
* show interest in what your partner says
* give examples and reasons for what you say
* give your partner a chance to speak.

■ Useful phrases

Questions	I like . . . , do you? What about you? What do you think about . . . ?
Continuing the conversation	That's interesting because . . . And another thing I like is . . .
Agreeing	So do I. Me too! I agree with you about that.

This worksheet is based on the whole PET for Schools Speaking test.

Try this quiz and find out.

How well do you know the Speaking test?

■ Task One

 Now watch the whole test again.

For each question choose the best answer – A, B or C.

1. How long is the Speaking test?
   A 8–10 minutes
   B 10–12 minutes
   C 12–14 minutes

2. How many parts does the Speaking test have?
   A 2
   B 3
   C 4

3. How many examiners are there?
   A 1
   B 2
   C 3

4. How many students are there?
   A Only one
   B Usually two
   C Always three

■ Task Two

Match the parts of the test (1–4), with the things you have to do (A–H).
You can use the letters more than once.

Part 1. _____ _____ _____ _____

Part 2. _____ _____ _____

Part 3. _____ _____

Part 4. _____ _____ _____

A	Spell your name.
B	Talk about people in an imaginary situation.
C	Answer the examiner's questions.
D	Talk to your partner.
E	Talk about a photograph.
F	Talk about yourself.
G	Ask your partner questions.
H	Talk on your own.

Photo B

Photo C